TOUGH GUIDES

HOW TO SURVIVE IN THE OCEAN

LOUISE SPILSBURY

WAYLAND
www.waylandbooks.co.uk

First published in Great Britain in 2018 by Wayland

Produced for Wayland by Calcium Creative Ltd
Editors: Sarah Eason and Jennifer Sanderson
UK Editor: Sarah Ridley
Designer: Simon Borrough
Cover design: Cathryn Gilbert

ISBN: 978 1 5263 0910 5
10 9 8 7 6 5 4 3 2 1

Wayland, an imprint of
Hachette Children's Group
Part of Hodder and Stoughton
Carmelite House
50 Victoria Embankment
London EC4Y 0DZ

An Hachette UK Company
www.hachette.co.uk
www.hachettechildrens.co.uk

Printed and bound in China

Photo credits: Cover: Shutterstock: Keren-seg, Willyam Bradberry. Inside: Dreamstime: Cornelius20 10l, 22l, Matthew Trommer 21t; Shutterstock: Rich Carey 6l, 18l, Cbpix 18c, Clearviewstock 17c, Djgis 11c, Undersea Discoveries 19t, Tom Dowd 12cr, Elena Elisseeva 10c, Idreamphoto 14c, Chaikovskiy Igor 6c, Irabel8 20c, Andrew Jalbert 4c, Juhana Lampinen 22cr, Iakov Kalinin 4l, 16l, 28l, DJ Mattaar 13t, William Attard McCarthy 7t, PhotoHappiness 4tr, Jason Patrick Ross 27cl, Lisa S. 16c, Keren-seg 14l, 26l, Galushko Sergey 12l, 24l, Shotgun 24c, AntonSokolov 8cl, Kayros Studio 8br, Tandemich 8l, 20l, Guido Vrola 9c, Wonderisland 5tl, Worldswildlifewonders 15t; US Coastguard: Petty Officer 3rd Class Brandyn Hill 23c, U.S. Army photo by Arthur McQueen 28cl; US Navy: Mass Communication Specialist 3rd Class Heidi McCormick 29tl, Mass Communication Specialist 2nd Class Bryan Weyers 25t.

CONTENTS

SURVIVAL!

We live on a blue planet. About three-quarters of Earth's surface is covered by seas and oceans. Every day thousands of people work on the ocean, travel across it or visit it to go sailing, diving, fishing or swimming. The ocean is wild and beautiful, but it can also be one of the most dangerous and challenging places on Earth.

shipwreck

SHIPWRECKS
WHAT: sunken ships on the ocean floor
HOW MANY: more than 3 million worldwide

Fierce storms can send huge waves crashing into a boat and even sink it. To survive on the ocean, people have to stay afloat, keep warm, find water and food and escape the hungry jaws of ocean monsters, such as the great white shark! How do people survive when they come face to face with these dangers?

TOUGH TIP

Watch out for oceanic whitetip sharks. Food is scarce for these hunters, so they make a meal of whatever they can find, including ship and plane disaster victims.

MOKEN PEOPLE
WHAT: the Moken dive for fish off islands in Myanmar and Thailand
HOW: Moken people see twice as well underwater as other people!

A SINKING SHIP

If a ship starts to sink, it is vital to stay calm. People who panic make mistakes, so take a few deep breaths and get to the ship's deck as quickly as you can. Send out a **Mayday** call, which is a radio message to say you are in trouble and you need help. Make sure you say who you are and where you are as clearly as you can.

stormy seas

STORMS AT SEA

WHAT: on average, two large ships sink worldwide every week

HOW: most shipwrecks are caused by storms

sinking boat

If you must **abandon** the ship, find a **life jacket** and put it on. Collect some emergency items for the life raft, such as food, water and a first-aid kit. Load these into the life raft carefully and quickly, and make sure you escape before the ship goes down!

TOUGH TIP

Some people say ships do not suck people down with them when they sink, but survivors who have escaped sinking ships say it does happen. Do not take any chances. Move away from a sinking ship quickly.

SINKING SHIPS

WHAT: sinking ships often roll onto one side as they sink
ACTION: watch out for objects sliding around and hold onto the sides of the ship to avoid slipping

7

STAYING AFLOAT

The biggest risk in the ocean is **drowning**. If you are not in a life raft it is vital to stay on top of the water. A simple life jacket can save your life. It helps you to float and it keeps your head above water. No life jacket? Hold onto something that is floating by, such as a log or a lifebelt.

life jacket

LIFE JACKET
WHAT: helps to keep you afloat
HOW: life jackets are filled with a light material, such as foam, or air

Swimming is hard work, so if you do not have a life jacket, float on your back with your arms and legs spread out. This will keep your face out of the water and you may even be able to sleep for short periods of time.

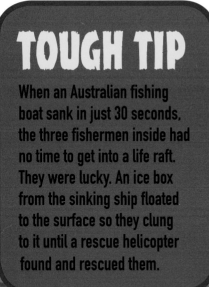

lifebelt

LIFEBELT
WHAT: can keep you afloat and help others rescue you
HOW: many are attached to a rope that is used to pull people to safety

SALTY WATER

No human can survive without water for more than three days, but you should never drink seawater. The salt in seawater can make you ill and even kill you. To survive you need to catch rainwater in your hands or any container you can find. You can also use a T-shirt or a ship's sail to catch this life-giving freshwater.

catching rainwater

WATER
FACT: two-thirds of the human body is water, a third solid material
THREAT: you need to drink 2 litres of water a day

This expert survival tip turns seawater into drinking water. Put seawater into a cup and stand it in an empty container. Wrap clear plastic over the top so that heat from the sun **evaporates** some of the seawater. When **water vapour condenses** on the plastic, it leaves the salt behind and freshwater drips into the container.

Use the sun!

TOUGH TIP

Stop eating. If you have food but no water, do not eat. Your body uses a lot of water to process your food, so eating makes **dehydration** even worse. It is possible to survive longer without food than without water.

SALTWATER
PROBLEM: seawater is too salty to drink
ACTION: when sunlight evaporates seawater the salt is left behind

CATCHING FISH

The ocean is full of fish that provide food for many of the world's people, but be careful which ones you try to catch. The long tentacles of a jellyfish can give a killer sting and some fish have spikes that can poison you. Luckily, in the middle of the ocean, most fish are safe to eat.

flying fish

FLYING FISH
SIZE: grows up to 45 cm long
HOW TO CATCH THEM: may leap out of the water and land in boats

mackerel **shoal**

Use any cloth you have to make a fishing net. Hold it underwater and scoop it upwards quickly to trap a fish. Bend a wire to make a fishing hook and tie it to a shoelace. Put tiny fish on the hook as **bait** to catch a larger fish.

TOUGH TIP

Dead fish rot fast, so make your own dried fish snacks. Dried fish are safe to eat for several days. Remove the bones and guts as soon as you catch the fish. Then cut the fish into thin strips and hang them up to dry in the air.

MACKEREL
SIZE: grows up to 41 cm long
HOW TO CATCH THEM: use a strip of fish as bait

13

CATCHING SEAFOOD

The deep blue ocean is bursting with life and fish are not the only choice of food. Sea turtles are easy to catch because they swim to the surface every few minutes to breathe, but try to avoid eating them because they are **endangered**. Seaweed is salty and tough, but it is good to eat as long as you have lots of drinking water.

sea turtle

SEA TURTLE
SIZE: grows up to 117 cm long
WHAT: it is illegal to eat sea turtles in many countries because they are dying out

seaweed

All birds are safe to eat so catch any seabirds that you can. Many seabirds feed on the ocean's surface so if you stay quiet they may land close by. If one lands on your life raft you might be able to grab it, or spear it using a knife tied to an oar.

SEAWEED
WHAT: eat only living seaweed
USE: can be eaten raw or as a boiled vegetable

TOUGH TIP

Three boys lost in the Pacific Ocean survived for 50 days before they were spotted by a fishing boat. They lived on rainwater, coconuts and a type of seabird that they caught when it landed on their boat. They killed the bird and ate it raw.

FINDING YOUR WAY

In the middle of the ocean all you can see around you is deep blue water, so how do you find your way? In the past sailors used the position of the sun, moon, and stars in the sky to **navigate**, but this takes skill. At night a distant, flashing light could be a lighthouse so aim for that.

message in a bottle

MESSAGE IN A BOTTLE
WHAT: put a message in a bottle and toss it out to sea
WHY: in 2011 a ship's crew threw a message in a bottle out to sea. The message was found and they were rescued

Do not miss out on the chance of rescue. Watch for signs that you are drifting close to land. Deep water is a dark green-blue colour and shallow water is lighter, which may mean land is near. Watch birds, too. There are usually many more birds near land than over the open ocean.

the night sky

NORTH STAR
WHAT: the most important star for navigation
WHY: an imaginary line drawn from this star to the nearest point on the **horizon** shows the direction north

SHARK ATTACK!

Large, sharp-toothed sharks are the most frightening animals in the ocean. These torpedo-shaped fish have powerful tails that push them through water at high speeds. Great white sharks are the deadliest. They swim up from below and bite into **prey** with a mouthful of 300 saw-like teeth.

reef shark

REEF SHARK
SIZE: up to 1.8 m long
THREAT: attacks swimmers that it mistakes as prey

18

tiger shark

I SURVIVED

For 13-year-old Bethany Hamilton a day at the beach in Hawaii almost ended in disaster. She was surfing when a tiger shark suddenly darted up and bit off her left arm. Bethany escaped and managed to use her right arm to swim to safety. Since she recovered, she has became a top class surfer.

If sharks see or hear something in the water they investigate, so do not kick and splash around too much. Sharks are also attracted to blood, so if you are injured try to stay out of the water. If you are attacked, kick or punch the shark in the nose and swim away!

TIGER SHARK

SIZE: grows to about 4 m long, can weigh more than 600 kg

THREAT: sharp teeth and powerful jaws can kill

STORMS AT SEA

Ocean storms can be terrifying. Howling winds can tear off parts of a ship and whip up huge waves, which toss boats around like toys. Winds can also wash people off boats into the rough sea. The best way to survive a storm at sea is to avoid it. Do not set out if a storm is on the way.

huge ocean wave

MONSTER WAVE
SIZE: can be 30 m high
THREAT: can **capsize** and sink boats and ships at sea

hurricane seen from space

TOUGH TIP

If you are in a life raft when a storm hits, you should be able to ride over high waves safely. Make sure that you close the raft covers and flaps to keep out as much water as possible.

Hurricanes are the most dangerous storms of all. Hurricane winds form over warm oceans and spin around and around in a spiral at high speeds. The centre, or eye, of a hurricane can be calm but its winds can create enormous waves. Some waves can be as tall as a three-storey building!

HURRICANE
WIND SPEED: up to 321 km/h
THREAT: can damage and sink ships at sea

TOO HOT, TOO COLD

With the sunlight reflecting off large areas of flat water, it can get very hot on the ocean. Skin burns quickly out at sea and getting too hot makes people very ill. Try to make a cover from sails or cloth to shade you from the sun. If it is very hot, making your clothes wet can help you to keep cool.

protect your eyes

SUN SAFETY
THREAT: invisible **ultraviolet (UV) rays** in sunlight burn and damage skin
ACTION: wear sunglasses and clothing to cover yourself

If you are in the water, cold is a real danger. The best thing to do is hold your knees up to your chest with your legs crossed. This is called the HELP (Heat Escape Lessening Position) and it helps your body to hold onto its warmth for longer.

If you are stranded in a life raft on a cold ocean it is important to keep dry because being wet will make you feel colder. Cover up with blankets, huddle together with other people, or flap your arms and move about until a rescue boat arrives.

sea rescue practice

HELP
FACT: you lose about 50 per cent of your body heat through your head
ACTION: use the HELP position to keep your head out of the water

PIRATES!

Long ago, fierce pirates attacked sailing ships with cannons and pistols. They used daggers and swords to frighten crews into handing over their **cargo**. Ships today are bigger, safer and faster, but pirates are still a real danger. Pirates often attack at night and hold the crew at gunpoint while they steal money, cargo, televisions and clothes.

skull and crossbones flag

SKULL AND CROSSBONES
IN THE PAST: used by pirates to scare people
TODAY: the symbol means something is dangerous, such as poison

US Navy captures modern-day pirates

Today some pirates steal people, too. They **kidnap** people from their boats and hold them to **ransom** for large sums of money. The best way to survive a pirate attack is never to get into it. Before you travel on the ocean, find out if the area is safe.

TOUGH TIP

In 2005 Jay Barry and his partner were on a trip around the world when they were attacked by armed pirates. When Barry saw four pirates speeding towards him, he rammed his ship at full speed into their boat. The shocked pirates turned and left, and Barry lived to tell the tale!

MODERN-DAY PIRATES

WHAT: pirates **hijack** ships off the coast of Africa and elsewhere
WHEN: the 21st century

25

STRANDED

Ocean dangers do not end when survivors reach an island. People can be injured or killed when boats hit jagged rocks or **coral reefs**, so try to land on sandy beaches when waves are gentle. Once ashore, your first job is to find fresh water. If there is no stream, collect coconuts as they contain lots of coconut water and fill you up, too.

desert island

DESERT ISLAND
WHAT: coconut palms grow on many desert islands
HOW: coconuts float across oceans and wash up on islands where they grow into trees

You will also need to build a shelter. A roof of branches and leaves protects you from the sun and rain. You could use wood or the life raft as a floor to keep you off the ground and away from deadly scorpions and snakes!

TOUGH TIP

Build a fire. You can use a fire to cook fish, boil water, keep you warm and it can help you get rescued! Keep piles of wood nearby so you can light them quickly, to act as a signal when you see an aeroplane or ship.

fire signal

FIRE SIGNAL
WHAT: the best way to signal for help in the dark
HOW: build three fires in a triangle. This is an international distress signal

RESCUED!

It is a real challenge to survive on the ocean. If you know how to find food and water and keep safe, you could stay alive until a rescue boat finds you. This can take a long time, so keep cheerful by singing, telling stories and making plans for the future.

helicopter rescue

RESCUE HELICOPTER
SIZE: about 21 m long
ACTION: lowers a cable to lift people out of the water

lifted to safety

Being rescued is the final challenge. Rescue is difficult and dangerous in rough ocean waves. Helicopters drop rescue swimmers into the ocean who battle through strong seas to reach survivors. Survivors are lifted to safety on a long cable that dangles from the helicopter high above the stormy seas.

RESCUE SWIMMER
PROBLEM: lifting an injured person to safety
ACTION: rescue swimmer lifts the victim in a lift strap that goes under his or her arms

GLOSSARY

abandon To leave a thing or place.

bait Food put on a hook or in a net to attract and catch fish.

capsize When a boat turns over in the water.

cargo The goods (things) carried by a ship or plane.

condense Change from a gas into a liquid.

coral reef Rock-like structure built by tiny ocean animals.

dehydration Illness caused by lack of drinking water.

drowning Dying underwater because you cannot breathe.

endangered Describes a type of animal that is at risk of extinction – dying out completely.

evaporate Change from a liquid into a gas.

hijack To stop and steal a boat or other vehicle.

horizon The line where the sky meets the land or the sea.

hurricane A violent storm with very strong, very fast spinning winds.

kidnap To hold someone against their will.

life jacket A jacket that fills with air, or is filled with a very light material, to help you float on water.

Mayday The radio signal for help used by ships and planes all over the world.

navigate To find one's way around.

prey An animal that is hunted and eaten by other animals.

ransom Money paid to free a kidnapped person.

shoal A large number of fish swimming together.

ultraviolet (UV) rays Invisible rays given off by the sun that can hurt your skin and eyes.

water vapour Water in a gas form.

30

FURTHER READING

Jinny Johnson, *The Open Ocean (Water Worlds)*
Franklin Wattts, 2012

Izzi Howell, *Ocean (Fact Cat)/Seas and Oceans (Fact Cat)*
Wayland, 2016, 2017

Louise and Richard Spilsbury, *Oceans of the World* series
Heinemann Educational Books, 2015

WEBSITES

The BBC have many sites about oceans, including 'What is an ocean habitat?' at:
www.bbc.co.uk/guides/zsfkd2p
and BBC Nature Open Oceans, where you can find out about the animals that live in the open ocean at:
http://www.bbc.co.uk/nature/habitats/Pelagic

Dive into National Geographic UK's Ocean Facts! at:
www.natgeokids.com/uk/discover/geography/general-geography/ocean-facts/#!/register

INDEX